# *SOULSCAPES:*

## *Human Heart and Countenance*

# SOULSAPES:

## Human Heart and Countenance

by

Sheilah R. Craft

Little Butterfly

Little Butterfly

The short stories in this collection are the original creative works of the author. All characters are fictitious or are used fictiously. Any resemblance to actual events or persons, living or dead, is entirely coincidental.



First Little Butterfly edition November 2014

ISBN-13: 978-0692332573

ISBN-10: 069233257X

The soul's joy lies in doing.

--Percy Bysshe Shelley

# CONTENTS

# AUTHOR'S NOTES

"The Visit" was written in 1992, the product of my intense admiration of the poet Percy Bysshe Shelley and the thought of what it would be like to meet him.

"The Conversation" was written on September 24, 1996, six days before the 41st anniversary of James Dean's death. September 30 is also my birthdate, a fitting time for nostalgia.

"Carolina Blues" is the oldest story in this volume, written in 1989. Although it has nothing in common with the song, I was inspired to write this story after listening to the Phil

Everly composition "Charleston Guitar."

"All of My Life" is a very recent story, one I wrote with the challenge to write a complete short story that contained only 1000 words—not one less nor one more.

"Tommy" is the result of another recent challenge, this one to write a character sketch that relied not on physical description but on inner thought—memories—in the space of a mere 500 words.

"Progeny of Heaven" was written in 1993, inspired by the idea of atonement for a great affront done to God and humankind.

# The Visit

The Italian sun was awakening in the sky, trying to find a comfortable position from which to begin the day. I call it the Italian sun, not because Italy possesses a different sun than the rest of the earth--it is just that the sun in Italy possesses a quality that is found nowhere else on earth. In the few days I have been here I have discovered that everything in Italy is of a more magical and majestic quality. There is nothing that is reminiscent of another country, there is nothing commonplace--everything is unique, singular.

Since my first morning here I have felt Italy's magic within me. As a consequence, my habits have changed; for instance, I now arise before dawn and spend most of the day working. Before I came here, I was far less disciplined, working whenever the urge flowed through me. When I say I spend most of the day working, it isn't meant that I have an eight-hour job to attend, with a boss and a time-card. My profession, as I refer to it, is that of writing.

My specialties are stories, pieces that come to me in flashes of inspiration. It has always come easy to me, writing has; I "see" each story in my mind, image by image, as I write it down. The process is like seeing a movie project itself on a screen in my mind. All I have to do is transcribe the action, dialogue, and plot as they are revealed to me.

It has long been my custom to have a notebook and pen with me at all times, no matter where I am going or what I am doing, for I never know when the movies will begin. Since arriving in Italy, though, I have established a routine: I arise early, set out for a quiet spot and begin writing. I usually write straight through until the evening shadows begin stretching lazily over the grass. I have, in just a few days, already filled one notebook with stories. The Muse has been working me overtime.

On this day I found myself drawn to a distant hill, for what reason I didn't know--perhaps only because it was an intriguing, solitary place among the bustle of late twentieth-century Rome. I knew from the moment I stepped out of the boarding house in which I was staying, and saw the hill way off in the distance, that it was where I wanted to go.

I set off, twisting and turning down little alleyways and avenues, drawing ever closer to my destination; as I did, the hill--lush and green--looked so majestic standing there against the rosy sky. And so alive, as if it could move of its own volition. I breathed deeply, the air becoming clearer, crisper, fresher as I reached the foot of the hill. I stood there, at the bottom, for a long moment, just savoring the sight, wanting to capture it forever in my memory, like a violet pressed between the pages of a book.

I climbed up the side, almost afraid to let my feet crush the dark green growth beneath them. It felt sacrilegious to tramp over the hill, for it looked so undisturbed, so fresh and wild, in the midst of this ancient city—I felt as if I were the first person to desecrate the mound of earth by traipsing over her. Of course, I reasoned, in all these hundreds of years, I wasn't.

Reaching the apex, though, my mind ceased its anxiety. I stood there, bewitched by the view. It was spectacular. I was so glad that I had come there. I turned slowly, examining each angle. Suddenly, I was paralyzed, stunned. Afar off, in the distance, was the Protestant Cemetery. I caught my breath, not knowing exactly how I should feel. It was a place of death, yet filled with exquisite beauty.

Finally, I regained my composure and sat down. I opened my notebook and uncapped my pen, but no words came. I only sat there, too aware of the Tomb of Cestius, the pyramid standing tall and haughty there in the cemetery.

I took a deep breath and forced myself to write, like a demon possessed, fast, frantic, the words pouring from me, until finally my hand was exhausted and cramped. I don't know how long I had been writing, though there were twenty-three filled pages. I was startled.

I skimmed the pages I had filled, discovering that I had, apparently, written another story, and in much less time than I normally did, though I didn't even remember turning the pages. I began to read it with interest—and curiosity. Clearly this story had come from my subconscious, and I was anxious to read it.

I don't know when I first became aware of the shadow that fell across my notebook, which was spread open over my knees. I finally looked over my shoulder; standing there, behind me, was a man, looking down at the notebook and reading my story along with me. I made a move to stand, annoyed at his intrusion, when he quietly said, "No, please, finish the story first."

Strangely, I did just that, and was somewhat surprised with myself. I would have expected my reaction to his effrontery to have been anger or indignation. Instead, I was calm, unperturbed. When I—we—came to the end of my story, I found him seating himself beside me. Give him credit, I thought; at least he hadn't used one of the standard come-on lines—at least his approach was original.

When I finally looked at him, I was more than amazed—I was numbed. He seemed to be an angel, an effectual angel, come to bless earth with his presence. He was dressed stylishly, fashionably, but with a careless manner.

The shoulders were stooped, as if he spent too much time bent over his work. His sandy-colored hair fell over his forehead and tumbled down his shoulders in windblown and disarrayed curls and waves. His dark blue eyes were deep and mesmerizing. In one short instant he had me completely captive under his spell.

I could only stare at him, thrilled and blessed to have him sitting with me. I was speechless, too overcome with emotion to speak. He smiled at my reaction, pleased but somewhat embarrassed. He was the one to open our conversation by asking simply, "How long have you been in Rome?"

"This is my fourth day."

"Then you have not yet seen the wonders of Rome. This city has remained the world's capital. Rome's palaces and temples are more glorious than those of any other city. But it's ruins are ever more glorious than they. You have much yet to experience here."

I smiled, knowing well the fullness of his love for Italy. "I have already seen Rome's most magnificent possession. It is a sight by which expression is overpowered—which words cannot convey."

He laughed, knowing better than I the source of the words I had spoken. "I am flattered that you remember my words on the merits of Rome's scenery. But, pray tell me--to which of Rome's many treasures are you referring?" His eyes were on mine, earnest and interested.

I can only assume that my own eyes were full of all the admiration I felt when I replied, "Why, you, of course." I knew I had embarrassed him immensely, for his eyes lowered and his cheeks were tinged with pink. I took his hand in both of mine, and said, "It's true. I have always greatly admired your work—and you. You're the reason I came to Rome in the first place."

He looked up again, a smile on his lips. He was not used to praise, for his work had been largely condemned by his own countrymen, contemporaries, and peers. It was important to me for him to know how much he meant to me.

"If you came here just to see me, why have you not yet been to visit me?"

Now I looked down; I didn't want him to see the tears that had suddenly formed in my eyes. I cleared my throat before I dared to speak. "Because I wasn't ready yet."

"Ready for what?"

"I-I wasn't prepared yet to see you there."

I was warmed and touched by the tender squeeze he gave my hand; and by the gentleness with which he raised my head so that my gaze met his. I saw the empathetic pain in his own eyes when he saw the tears drifting down my cheeks. His fingers were so soft, warm and gentle as he caressed the tears away. He pulled a white linen handkerchief from his pocket and handed it to me; I wiped my eyes and face, enchanted by his concern and gallantry. We sat in silence for a moment before I mumbled, "I'm sorry."

"You have no need to apologize." He turned then, and looked down at the cemetery, his arm linked through mine. He sighed deeply, then said, "The cemetery of the

Protestants is romantic and lovely: under the pyramid which is the tomb of Cestius and the mossy walls and towers, mouldering and desolate, which formed the circuit of ancient Rome. The cemetery is one with Nature—an open space among the ruins, covered in winter with violets and daisies. It is more beautiful than any other place on earth."

I looked down at it, the pyramid standing tall and proud, like an eternal guardian watching over the graves in the cemetery. I was enthralled by his description, his words having replaced my pain and fear with awe and wonder. Then I looked at him, his face so full of peace and serenity. He felt my gaze and smiled at me; we were like two children sharing a special secret. "Did it make you fall in love with death?," I asked softly.

He grinned, amused. "I think it did, at that."

"I'm glad you're happy there."

"Does it really matter to you if I am or not?" He was teasing me now, those blue eyes gleaming.

"Of course it does."

"I would have to be, being in so sweet a place."

There was nothing else for us to say at that moment, so we sat in comfortable silence, relishing the view below us and the sounds and smells of Nature around us. I lay my head on his shoulder, our hands clasped between us. It felt as if we had known one another forever; in many ways we had.

We sat there, absorbing the essence of Italy—and of each other—until the sun began her deliberately slow walk home for the evening. I raised my head then, breathing deeply. "Spring in Rome is a miraculous season."

He was staring straight ahead, but squeezed my hand in agreement. "The bright blue sky of Rome, and the effect of the vigorous awakening of spring in this divinest climate, and the new life with which it drenches the spirits even to intoxication—it is an inspiration to the soul."

I looked at him once more, completely amazed and awed at his presence. His appeal was ineffable, and so very potent and powerful. Spending the day with him had been a dream come true. "Thank you."

"For what?"

"For everything: for being here, for sharing yourself with me, for the most wonderful day of my life."

"I, too, enjoyed today. It has been a very long time since I have talked with someone this way."

He stood up then, and my heart fell—I knew he was leaving, and I didn't want him to. I wanted him to stay there forever. I knew he couldn't, though, and that he had to return to his world. I felt tears stinging my eyes again. I held his hand tightly, unable to speak, but hoping he would know how I felt.

He squeezed my hand once more, and I knew I had conveyed my emotions to him. I looked into those blue eyes as he said, "I must walk forth into the purple and golden light of an Italian evening."

He placed something in my hand as he turned away. I stood there, watching his graceful descent down the hill. When he reached the base he turned his head and called, "Come and visit me."

I swallowed my tears and yelled back, "I will."

He smiled and nodded, and walked on toward his destination. I kept my focus on him as tears fell unchecked down my cheeks. Finally, as he stood beneath the pyramid, he turned and waved. I raised my hand in an answering valediction—and that's when I saw the violet there. When I looked at the cemetery again, he was gone.

Smiling, I bent down and picked up my notebook. I placed the violet between two of the pages and stuffed the handkerchief in my pocket as I set off down the side of the hill. As I walked, I knew where I would be going the next morning—and every morning. I had no need for the spirit of solitude any longer, for I had found the brother of my soul.

## *The Conversation*

Catherine stood at the window looking out at the early morning of another new day. It was cold. It was raining. It was dark and dreary. This new day did not fill her with happiness or thankfulness even though it was her birthday, and it wasn't because she was depressed over becoming another year older. It wasn't even really because of the rain, even though it reminded her of a night so long ago. No, her sadness had been with her for more than forty years, for most of her life.

Her sorrow came from long ago and far away—or did it? Wasn't it always with her?

She recalled her eighteenth birthday, September 30, 1955, the day she officially became an adult. It had begun happily enough, with her few close friends gathered for fun and food in her New York apartment. They had shared so much laughter that day in 1955. It had been so carefree and happy.

Suddenly, Cathi felt a horrible knife of pain slice through her. She heard one of the guys asking what time it was, shouting to be heard over the laughter and the radio. Someone shouted back, "5:45. Why? Got somewhere else to be?" That was the last thing Cathi heard before she felt herself falling and the world go completely dark.

Tears slid down Catherine's cheeks just like the rain slid down the window pane, as she pulled a yellowed notebook from her desk and opened it. As she read, her memory traveled back in time. . . . .

It was cold. It was raining. It was dark and dreary. It was Cathi's first day in New York City and she was walking down Broadway trying to find a place to stay for the night. So far, every place she'd entered had been full—if she heard, "Sorry, lady, no vacancies," one more time, she knew she would scream. Or cry. She was so frustrated. So cold. So wet. So depressed. And so very tired. She had had such plans, dreams, and expectations about moving to New

York. It wasn't supposed to be *this* way.

As she fought back her tears and her self-pity, Cathi noticed an all-night diner on the opposite corner. She walked across the street, already too wet and too cold to worry about mud puddles and splashing cars. At least she would have a place to rest and get something hot to drink. She needed a cup of coffee—desperately. She knew she wouldn't be able to stay awake much longer without the caffeine.

However, her spirits fell yet again when she entered and saw that every table was taken. She slumped against the wall in despair, forcing back the tears with immense effort. She did not want to cry—not here, not now, not in front of all these strangers, like some lost little girl. But that's exactly what she felt like: lost, lonely, and alone.

Just as she was steeling herself to go back outside, into the cold, dark, rain, Cathi felt something hit her. She looked down and saw a crumpled paper napkin at her feet. Suddenly, another paper ball flew at her, and she looked up to see someone beckoning her from the back of the diner. Hesitantly, she picked up her bag and walked to the booth, to find herself looking down at the top of a mussed blond head surrounded by a halo of cigarette smoke. She stood there, not sure what was expected of her, when a mumbled voice suddenly asked, "Aren't you gonna sit down?"

As she took off her sopping coat, hung it over the seat, and slid onto the bench, she said a heartfelt, "Thank you." She extended her right hand to him and then said, "I'm Cathi." He grunted in response, but never moved. So she simply folded her arms against her chest, trying vainly to keep warm.

They sat in awkward silence for several minutes, until a waitress appeared and asked Cathi what she wanted. She gratefully ordered coffee and a salad. As lightning flashed in the dark sky outside the window, she hugged her arms closer, chills shooting icicles through her. Suddenly a heavy leather jacket was thrown across the table at her. She didn't move--she simply stared at him in amazement.

"You gonna put it on, or what?" he mumbled.

"Thank you."

She wasn't sure what to think of this strange creature sitting hunched across from her. Or was *she* the strange one? She considered herself intelligent and possessing at least a degree of common sense. She spoke in complete, correct sentences and in a clear, distinct voice. This boy, on the other hand, had so far managed to execute two garbled questions and a few grunts of acknowledgment.

Somehow he had made her feel stupid and inadequate. Cathi did not understand this.

She wondered if most New Yorkers were like him. Listening to the mostly well-enunciated, clear speech filling the diner, she doubted it. She doubted that there was anyone like him, anywhere. Just then the waitress placed Cathi's salad and coffee in front of her, interrupting her thoughts. She smiled up at the woman and thanked her, getting a surprised, "You're welcome," in return.

As she picked up her fork, Cathi saw his face for the first time. He was staring at her, his brow wrinkled in fascination. She was mesmerized. He was beautiful. His eyes were a deep, dark, intense blue, his lips were full, his cheekbones high. The tousled blond hair, the cigarette drooping at the corner of his mouth, and the wrinkled shirt gave him an air of not so much carelessness as an aura of someone with far more important concerns.

Suddenly he was no longer a sloppy, unkempt, impolite oaf; he was a man of intensity, of deep thought, of seriousness. Her perception of him had changed drastically with one look at his face, his eyes. Those eyes. They weren't the eyes of an unintelligent slob. They were the eyes of an intelligent artist. She somehow instinctively knew he was an artist, that he lived through and by his creativity.

That mumble suddenly cut into her thoughts, almost but not quite breaking the spell. "You a rabbit or one of those vegetarian freaks?"

Without losing a beat, she replied,

"A rabbit."

For the first time since she'd joined him he smiled, and giggled a little-boy giggle. His beautiful face was transformed. The sullenness was replaced with mirth.

He stopped giggling, leaned far back in his seat, and asked, "No, really, are you?"

"Am I what? A rabbit?"

"No. A veggie eater."

"Yes, I'm a vegetarian."

"Why?" He was serious and interested, and he wasn't mumbling any longer. Apparently, when he had something important enough to say he said it distinctly.

"Because I don't want animals to die simply so I can eat their dead bodies. I feel that their lives are far too important for that."

"What if you were stranded in the woods and you had to kill a squirrel or rabbit to survive?"

"I wouldn't do it because it wouldn't be necessary."

"You'd die. You think an animal's life is more important than your own?"

"I think *all* life is important. And I wouldn't die. There is plenty to eat in the woods without killing an animal."

His face was wrinkled in childlike disbelief as he asked, "Like what?"

"There are lots of things: nuts, berries, pine needles, bark. . . ."

"Pine needles?! Bark?! You expect me to eat pine needles instead of rabbit? No one eats pine needles."

"I have. There's nothing wrong with pine needles. It's better than having the guilt of an innocent creature's blood on your soul."

"Why would you feel guilty for keeping yourself alive?"

"Is it right or moral to take one life for another? Murder is murder, whether you kill a rabbit or a man. The end result is still the same—you've taken a life."

"Killing a rabbit is different from killing a man."

Now it was her turn to ask the question, to force him to defend his point of view. "How so?"

He looked pleased by the challenge, as if he had wanted this reaction from her. "Because people are more important than rabbits."

"Are we really? Who says we are?" As he obviously struggled for an answer she took the opportunity to continue. "Just because people in the past have felt this way about the superiority of human life doesn't mean we have to blindly accept their opinions. We need to look within ourselves. We need to search our souls and our hearts and discover our own beliefs and feelings—on this and every other issue: politics, religion, love, equality. We need to discover what our personal beliefs and feelings are and then have the courage to remain true to and defend them."

He sat there for a long moment, staring at her, absorbing her intensity. He lit another cigarette, shrugged one shoulder, and merely said, "You're right."

She was pleasantly surprised. She knew that she was passionate about the issue, and knew that most people were not willing to listen to, let alone consider, her arguments. Not only had he listened—really listened—he had realized that his point of view was not the only one, that it probably wasn't truly his in the first place. She was satisfied that at least she had him rethinking his position. "Thank you."

"So. Is there anything else I can get you raving about?"

"I don't know. Why don't you try?"

Instead, he leaned back, his arms draped across the back of the bench, the cigarette dangling from the corner of his mouth. Through squinted eyes and a cloud of smoke he looked at her, stared at her, studied her.

"Do you always stare at people so intensely?" she asked.

"Usually. It's what I do."

"Excuse me?" She wasn't at all sure what he meant.

"I watch people. I read them. I take from them. I study life and I use life."

"Are you a writer?"

"I am an actor."

She had been right about him—he was an artist. He was in New York rather than California; that told her that he was serious about his craft, that he wasn't seeking fame and fortune so much as he was trying to feed a need within himself. She understood. That was why she had left everyone and everything behind and come to New York. New York was the place to be if you were committed to your inner voice, the one that told you, in no uncertain terms, what it was you were supposed to be doing. That was why thousands of painters, writers, dancers, and actors were living and struggling in New York City. That was why he was here, and that was why Cathi was here.

"How long have you been here?"

"A couple of years." He didn't volunteer anything further.

She refused to ask how he liked the city; if he had been here for two years then he at the least found it tolerable if not pleasant.

"You?"

She realized that he was asking her the same question. "Not very long at all—a couple of hours. Until I came in here, I was walking the streets looking for a room. All I've seen of the city so far are rain, cars, motel clerks who all speak the same language, people, cracked sidewalks, dark and lonely buildings, and this diner."

He raised an eyebrow in amusement and said, "Sounds like New York City on any day or night. You've seen it all."

She stared into the depths of her coffee cup and softly said, "I hope not."

"What were you expecting?"

"Expecting?" she repeated. She was silent, still peering into her cup, for a very long moment before she offered an answer. "I expected life, living, to permeate every core of the city at every moment."

"This *is* life, baby. Enjoy it while you can."

"No. What I saw out there this evening was not life, not even living."

"Then what do you call it, all those people crowding the sidewalks?"

"*That* is merely existing. Most of those people were enacting what, for them, is a daily ritual. They were going from work to home or from home to work. They follow the same carved-in-stone schedule every day without variation. They wake up, get ready, go to work, do some chores or stop off at a bar or a diner, go home, go to bed—and then repeat the procedures the next twenty-four hours. That isn't living, that is existing."

"What's the difference?"

She looked at him, puzzled. "Don't you know?"

He shrugged his shoulders. "Maybe, maybe not. Tell me how you define them."

"Living means you absorb everything around you, that you observe everyone and everything, that you learn from the past to influence the present and change the future. It means you are aware of every tiny sound made by nature, by the world we live in and its inhabitants. It means believing in something with every fiber of your being and having the courage to defend and stand up for that belief. It means that you don't follow the majority, that you aren't afraid to discover who you really are and let that person come alive. It means that you are attuned to your inner self, the one who tells you, without words, what your true mission on Earth is. It means that somehow, by following that voice, by being true to your unique self, by absorbing and observing, you make a difference. It doesn't matter how large or how small. The important thing is that you don't merely take from the world but that you give to the world.

"Those people out there were more like programmed robots than viable human beings. Not even the rain threw them off course. They were all on the same path, they seemed made from the same mold. Most of them center their worlds around their jobs, their calendars, their clocks. They don't observe or absorb, they don't discover who they really are, they don't hear that inner voice, they don't give back. They aren't aware of Earth's voices. They don't consider the world at large. They exist from minute to minute, hour to hour, day to day, doing what they have been led to believe they *have* to do. They probably will never make a difference on anyone outside of their immediate circle."

He had listened to her and watched her carefully as she spoke. "What about death? Everyone's going to die, so what does it really matter how each person spends their minutes and their hours? In the end, does any of it truly matter?"

"Of course it matters. Yes, each human being faces death, and we are aware of its imminence. But death merely ends the life on this planet anyway. Death kills the body but not the soul, not the essence of the person.

"It always saddens me to realize that there are thousands of people who will not be eternally remembered for what they did while alive. Once those who personally knew them are also dead, there is no one left to remember them.

But there are thousands more who are etched on the pages of eternal history, whose lives and works while alive remain vibrant forever, for each succeeding generation. These are the people who truly lived, who made a difference which reached far beyond even their comprehension."

"Like who?"

"Like Jesus, like Michelangelo, like Shakespeare, like Lincoln, Plato, Dickens, Tchaikovsky, Rousseau, Bach, Milton, Beethoven, Joan of Arc, de Vinci, and Shelley."

"What about the everyday people?"

"No one starts out known and appreciated and admired for his or her ideas and works. Each of those people began just as we all do, in relative obscurity, without fame or notoriety or attention. Jesus is the only one who gained attention at His birth. But each of these people gained fame and attention as their ideas and works were scattered among the people just like dead leaves on an autumn day."

"I think there's only one true form of greatness for man. If a man can bridge the gap between life and death. I mean, if he can live on after he's dead, then maybe he was a great man. To me, the only success, the only greatness, is immortality."

"Exactly. Some people strive for

that, others are not even conscious of it."

"I am. I want to live forever."

"How? What are you doing to make the kind of impact that gives birth to immortality?"

"I told you—I'm an actor."

"So are half of the people in New York."

"Yeah, but I'm different. I'm gonna be the best actor ever. I'm gonna make everyone sit up and notice me."

"I hope you get what you want and

expect."

"I will."

She gave him a little smile. "At least you have confidence in yourself."

"I think most creative people do. They have to. I mean, they know what they can do. They're aware of their talent. That in itself gives them some confidence." She didn't respond. "Don't you think?"

"I don't know. I suppose it depends on the person. Sure, all artists are aware of their talents—if they weren't, they wouldn't be using them.

But that doesn't necessarily equate confidence."

"Yeah, but when people are telling you they love you, when those who matter are telling you they think you're the best, that makes it worthwhile and gives you that confidence in yourself."

"What about the artists who never get feedback, whose works are not recognized until after their deaths? Their contributions and changes are still vital and effectual, and through them they gain their immortality."

"I don't know if it's worth it if you

have to wait until after you're dead to get fame and attention. I want it *now*, while I can appreciate it. I want my immortality to begin now, and I want to be aware of it."

"But as long as your message is given to the majority, as long as you accomplish some sort of positive change, it shouldn't matter. Is fame really so important that it should be someone's goal?"

He shrugged one shoulder in that casual manner of his and replied, "Sure it is. Everyone wants to be loved. It's human nature."

"But not all of the great people are loved while they're alive, at least not by the majority. No one did more for the world or effected more changes than Jesus, and he was not loved by everyone, especially not by those who mattered, as you call them. The men who made the important decisions are the ones who murdered Him. It was the same for Joan of Arc; she was murdered simply because of her beliefs and her conviction to them. But their messages, their beliefs, have remained vital and important for thousands of years. Each of them changed the world forever and became immortalized without having the love of the people in charge.

"All that matters is that each person does what he or she feels destined to do while giving to the world. If his or her work is valid it will be appreciated and perpetuated. It may not always happen when he or she wants it to, but it will happen."

Now he was silent, considering her words. "I see what you're saying, and it's not really that I disagree. It's just that I think people should know what others think of them when they're alive to hear it. I mean, if I open on Broadway tomorrow, and the critics and fans all say I'm the best actor ever, that I've given new life to a character, and I get run over and killed leaving the theater after the performance, what good was any of it? I'll never see the reviews, I'll never know what people thought of me as an actor. It won't mean anything."

"Yes, it will. If you were *that* good

that you brought something new and different to acting, then people will remember you. That kind of tremendous impact is not forgotten overnight. In fact, it probably makes the person an instant legend."

He looked at her through squinted eyes, his brow wrinkled in thought. "You think so?"

"Yes. Why? Are you thinking of jumping in front of a car after your opening night on Broadway?"

"I don't know." He said it so seriously that she looked shocked. He noticed and giggled that childish giggle. "Naw. Not me. I've got too much to do. But you believed I was thinking it, didn't you? Told you I'm good. I can make people believe anything. I can be anyone I choose to be."

"Are you ever truly yourself? If you're always pretending to be someone else, no one will ever get to know *you*."

"Exactly."

"Why should it be so hard to just be yourself with people? Don't you want people to judge you honestly, based on who you really are, rather than on false impressions?"

"No. If you knew me, you'd see why."

She noticed the glint in his eyes, the hint of a smile on his lips, and decided against answering the remark. He apparently enjoyed baiting people into debates and arguments, and she refused to play along any more. She enjoyed their repartee, but felt they had made their points. That left them surrounded by a web of silence and a cloud of smoke—he smoked constantly—while the talk and laughter from the other tables floated around them.

She also found herself wondering whether he had revealed his real self to her or whether he had been in character the entire time. She would probably never know, because she would probably never see him again. New York was such a huge, cavernous city, populated by thousands of bodies. They were only two of the many, and the chances of their paths crossing again were slim.

She knew, though, that she would remember him always--every strand of blond hair, every plane of his face, the smile, the frown, the wrinkled brow, the stooped shoulders, the cigarettes, the eyes. He would remain etched in her memory because he was unforgettable. She couldn't define what set him apart from all others, but she did know he had come into her life and made a lasting impression.

She would also recall that mumble, that giggle, that voice. She would hear them echoing in her memory decades in the future. There was no one else like him, that she knew with certainty. He would look and sound perfect on a stage, and she would cherish the opportunity to see him in his element. She hoped she someday had that chance.

Suddenly, that voice cut into her thoughts, breaking the chain. "You do it, too."

"Hmm? Do what?"

"Stare at people." As she looked down at the table and blushed, he said, "You've been staring at me for the past fifteen minutes. What's *your* excuse?"

"I'm sorry. I was just trying to figure you out. I was thinking how we will probably never see one another again, yet how important tonight has been."

"First of all, don't try to figure me out. No one can. No one. And that's the way I want it. I want to confuse people, I want to intrigue people. And why is tonight so important?"

"Because we've discussed some very relevant ideas. That's how things change; it isn't just through books.

We've shared opinions and thoughts, and we've argued about them. That's one of the most important things people can do, especially creative people."

He raised his eyebrows, his forehead wrinkling. She wasn't sure whether it was a sign of amusement or of challenge; either one was possible from him. "Is that all?"

Cathi couldn't look at him. Her heart was pounding in her chest. She hoped he hadn't been able to read her thoughts on her face, in her eyes. She quickly speared a wilting lettuce leaf with her fork and stuffed in her mouth, giving herself an instant excuse for not answering.

He didn't give up, though. "*I* wouldn't have anything to do with the way you're feeling, would I?"

Swallowing, she gained her composure and responded, "You're awfully sure of your charms, aren't you?"

He shrugged. "Why not? Women find me irresistible."

She looked around the diner. "Yes,

I can tell. They're throwing themselves at your feet."

He stuck his fingers in his water glass and flicked water at her face. She returned the gesture. As her hand was in mid-air he grabbed it and held it to his face, pressing her palm against his cheek. She was startled by this show of emotion, yet was reluctant to visibly react in any way, for fear of causing him to retreat into himself once more. This was what she had been waiting for: some sign, no matter how small, of the real person.

He held her hand for a long time, as if reliving a moment from his past, recalling in vivid details a precious memory. Finally he kissed her hand gently and let go of it as suddenly as he had grabbed it. Acting on impulse, she slowly pulled her hand away from his face and placed it on top of his hand. She was surprised that he did not pull away, for she would have expected him to rebuff any further signs of emotion.

They continued to sit in comfortable silence for several minutes, until the waitress came to their table and asked them if they wanted more coffee. Simultaneously, instinctively, inexplicably, they looked one another in the eyes and burst out laughing. The startled, offended waitress quickly walked away, mumbling something about lazy beatniks under her breath. They laughed even harder.

When they finally regained their composure and stopped laughing, they suddenly became aware that it was no longer raining. And that the sky was tinged with the palest pink as dawn drew ever closer to full bloom. They had spent most of the night at the booth, talking, arguing, playing, connecting.

He gulped down the last of his cold coffee and stretched languidly, his arms reaching the length of the bench. She knew their time together was almost over. She felt a painful prick of sadness, realizing that this complex person would probably never enter her life again. He gave her a little smile, as if sensing her thoughts and feelings.

He winked at her and said, "My bike is outside. Do you want a ride?"

She had never been on a motorcycle before, and had always refused rides offered by strangers, just as her parents had taught her. But she felt reckless and wild, willing to take a chance. Perhaps it was because this was her first full day in New York, maybe it was because it was her sixteenth birthday, or possibly it was because of him. It was probably a heady mixture of all three.

She instantly said, "Yes," stood up, and handed his jacket to him. She threw her coat on, tossed her bag onto her shoulder, and followed him. Her rain-washed coat and hair made the perfect complement to his wrinkled clothes and hair.

Sitting behind him, her arms tight around his waist, she told him she needed any motel or hotel with a vacancy. He drove as recklessly as he dressed, yet she never felt any fear or danger. He did not seem the kind to take unnecessary chances with his life—the present was too important to him. He lived for the moment.

Finally they stopped at a four-story

brick building with a "Vacancy" sign in the window. How he knew there was a vacancy there she didn't know, but she was grateful. She got off the bike and thanked him. He gave her a mock salute in reply.

As he gunned the motor, preparing to pull away and exit her life, he said, belatedly, "My name's Jim—James Dean. Look for it in lights, babe."

She watched him drive away, his blond hair blowing and his jacket ballooning as the wind whipped around him. She caught herself thinking that she wanted to record this night in her journal, preserving every tiny detail of their night together, of their conversations, of their shared yet unspoken moments of intimacy. This would be the first writing she would do in New York City.

She stepped into the motel and thought to herself that Jim was too ordinary a name for someone as extraordinary as he was. She had expected to hear a dramatic, even poetic, name, one that would demand attention. A name like Byron. Byron was the perfect name for him, for he was so much like the poet: charming yet aloof, self-assured yet scared, dangerous yet protective, beautiful, and forced by destiny to express himself to the world. She could only pray that he never met the same fate as the poet.

She smiled to herself as she climbed the stairs to her room, knowing that it would be hard for her to think of her Romantic hero—her Byron—as Jim. Unless she saw his name in lights, that is. And she knew that if she did she would instantly recall their night together in the diner. She would come to know him as everyone else would: as James Dean, the actor who was so good that he changed and affected the world unalterably.

Cathi closed her old journal and wiped a tear from her cheek. She tossed the notebook on the desk, next to a pile of manuscripts. She offered a smile toward Heaven as she softly said, "You got your wish, Jim."

## *Carolina Blues*

The lights were shining, the stars and moon were gleaming; nearly everyone and everything were asleep. Caroline Spencer was one of the few who were awake. She didn't like the night; once she was alone, in the quiet darkness, everything came flooding back. So, to keep the memories from bursting her internal dam, she spent her late night hours escaping.

Escaping with her guitar and her pen: Caroline wrote songs to soothe her aching spirit and heart. It was funny in a sad way, because Caroline had realized her musical and poetical potentials from Joseph. Tall, beautiful Joseph. Scared, unwilling Joseph. The man she so deeply loved, loved so much it hurt. However, Joseph was too afraid to let his heart conquer his mind, so now Caroline was alone--and lonely.

And she was remembering, whether she wanted to or not. Caroline suddenly jumped up and threw her pen across the room; it was the first available thing. It wasn't enough, though. Caroline couldn't stand it anymore, being between these four walls. So she grabbed her sweater and ran from her apartment and down the rickety stairs. She didn't care that she was probably waking everyone else. She had to get away.

She walked as fast as she could until her burning lungs forced her to slow down. Soon she found herself near King Street, and stopped in amazement; she hadn't realized she'd gone so far. Oh well, she was here, so why not enjoy it? She strolled down the sidewalk, taking in the serenity of the beautiful old buildings; why couldn't she feel like that, be like them? It wasn't fair, it just wasn't fair. As tears streamed down her cheeks, she ran. Suddenly she felt so totally alone, felt like she had to get far, far away. Get away from the past, the memories, the pain--and the future. She didn't know exactly where she wanted to be, just that she didn't want to be here any longer. If she kept running, maybe she'd be able to get away. . .maybe.

*Your lips were like wine,*

*But your heart was never mine;*

*You said you loved me--*

*So why did you have to be free?*

Caroline's voice carried and broke above the bittersweet chords of her guitar. This was her job; she'd gotten it from Joseph, too. When he'd left Caroline and Charleston, he'd left a spot at the club he'd played and sung at. Knowing how well Joseph had taught Caroline to write and play, the manager had asked her to fill the vacancy.

She'd been there every night since, singing her heart and soul out to anyone who came. It was her only way of staying close to him without any pain; the pain she sang away while she was on stage. It was here that she'd met and fallen in love with Joseph, at the corner table between his sets one night. Singing here was the only way she could face the ghosts that sat at the corner table. Without her music and her show, she'd have driven herself into the depths of depression.

She was never very far from the brink, anyway. Caroline hated the pain Joseph had caused her, but she didn't know how to get rid of it. Everything she saw somehow reminded her of it; everything she did was based on it. She survived on it: she lived it, breathed it, wrote it, sang it. It was almost as if she really didn't want to lose it, no matter how much she told herself she did.

It never helped, either, that the audience lavished her with praise. In her eyes the accolades were really for Joseph—since he had made her realize her talent and since her music was inspired by Joseph, the compliments were for him. It wasn't Caroline they liked so much as the pain she sang about. It was from Joseph, and it was all for him, too. Her life wasn't her own any more. She was no longer herself. The person she had been was sitting at that corner table, holding hands with the ghost she both loved and hated.

Three months later, still submerged in her routine of nighttime existence, Caroline was stopped by the club manager after her set one evening. He introduced her to a man in a three-piece suit who thrust a business card in her hand as he flashed her a smile. She looked at it in surprise; it said he was a record producer from New York. Her mind whirled dizzily as he said he'd like to take her to New York for an audition; he was sure he could get her a contract with a major label. She didn't have to answer him right away; he'd be at her next show to hear her decision.

That night, she walked to her room slowly, in a daze, a million questions murmuring in her head.

What was happening? Why to her? What should she do?

Closing her door, she sighed and sat down her guitar case. She went to the small bed and picked up her notebook and pen just as she always did. She started writing automatically; tonight it came easier than ever. The longer she wrote, the further away New York became. She was once more immersed in her life with Joseph.

As the sun rose and the city slowly came to life, so did Caroline. For the first morning in several months she went out for an early cup of coffee. Suddenly, the skyline in front of her was filled with tall buildings and dirty air. She began to think she could have it all: her music; the career Joseph had dreamed of—and Joseph. She hadn't been able to get him back by staying here; maybe leaving would somehow bring him to her once more. She had to try. So, she told the producer yes, and the next afternoon they were in his posh high-rise office.

Things happened fast for Caroline after that—faster than she'd ever imagined they could. She got her contract and began selecting songs with the producer for her album. He was amazed at how calm she always seemed to be: she never giggled or acted silly; she did nothing that indicated she was nervous or even excited. In fact, she never even smiled. Oh well, like the PR man had said, the image of a sullen, quiet loner of a rebel would be great for sales and publicity. Elusive and private as she was, she'd be sought by everyone. She was a PR rep's dream come true, and he didn't even have to do any of the footwork. It was already done by Caroline herself; he merely had to put the word out about this new sensation-in-the-making.

A sensation she became: Caroline's unique bluesy sound, with that melodramatic sadness, became an instant hit. She was in demand, big time. She accepted the fame and the attention as calmly as she had everything else. Her producer and her manager were still awed by her coolness; she was polite but never friendly, she answered the questions but she never revealed anything about herself. She was a master at it, a born natural. She had everybody eating out of her hand and begging for anything she would give them; she somehow managed to satisfy everyone while always leaving them wanting even more. None of it fazed her, though; she never cared. She constantly said her music was most important to her, that it was part of her mission—she just never told anyone that her mission was to get Joseph back, and that her music was the tool with which to accomplish it.

Her routine never changed, either—she spent her nights writing, filling notebook after notebook with those heartbreaker songs that were making an awful lot of people an awful lot of money. Soon she was opening for a top-name pop act, drawing as much of the audience as he was. She was everyone's darling, and everyone loved her—except Joseph. And until he did, she would never be whole again. She wanted him, she loved him desperately—and she looked for him everywhere she went.

She looked for Joseph in every city, in every club and arena, but she never saw him. Years passed before Caroline even really knew they had. Suddenly she was thirty and she realized in startled surprise that a decade—ten years—had gone by. Ten years of singing and writing—and searching for Joseph. But she'd never seen him. He had to be somewhere, anywhere, just so that she could find him, see him, hold him. Surely he'd known of her career by now; she'd expected him to show up one night, out of curiosity, if nothing else.

She felt so depressed and sad as she took the stage that night. Now the headliner, she shared the spotlight with no one. It didn't have to be that way, of course; the presents and flowers thrown on stage for her birthday that evening showed her how many people cared about her. Performers she'd worked with in the past had tried to get close to her, but she'd always turned them down immediately. Her manager had stopped lecturing her about the benefits of a relationship long ago; he stopped asking questions, too. Caroline's past was her own, and she didn't share it with anyone. She was her own person, independent and alone—and lonely.

She became more withdrawn with the passing of time. The only places people saw her anymore were on stage or in the studio. She was more of a loner than ever; she began disappearing for hours at a time in every city where they performed. She never told anyone where she was going or what she was doing, and they all knew not to ask. That didn't stop them from worrying, however. Sighing, her manager always excused her by saying that she was an artist, that all artists were crazy, and figured that as long as she always came back unharmed, he'd give her her eccentricities.

The year of her fifteenth anniversary in the business, the year she turned thirty-five, her manager booked her for a series of homecoming shows in Charleston. She had agreed with a careless shrug, but had fought back the tears. It would be the first time she'd been back since she'd gotten on the plane to New York.

Caroline arrived in Charleston to a parade and the biggest reception she'd ever gotten. They remembered her from the old club, they loved her, and they finally welcomed her home. She accepted their praise and their presents graciously, and with a sad smile.

Her shows there were the best of her career. No one knew it was because her heart was hurting so badly. She had no choice but to sing her blues with all the pain she felt. It was her professional triumph.

Early the next morning, before the sun was awake in the sky, she crept out of her hotel room. She went alone to the places of her past: her old apartment building, more run-down and shabby than ever; the old club where it had all begun, now boarded up and occupied only by the two ghosts who still sat at the corner table--she shuddered as she saw them through the dingy window.

She had searched the entire earth for Joseph, and she'd never found him. Perhaps if she started all over again she would. But where should she look? Everything was so different. Did she have a chance? Of course she did, just as much as she did anywhere else. So, she went to the little diner she'd gone to that morning fifteen years before and ordered a cup of coffee. She drank three as she waited for the library to open.

When it did, she was the first person there. She asked for the newspaper archives, and was led to them by a giggling young woman who repeated four times that it was an honor to have Caroline there. Caroline asked for the issues from the last fifteen years, and was presented them with a smile and a request to sign an autograph. Caroline did so quietly and dutifully, then was left alone to her task.

She began with the issue dated the afternoon of the day she'd gone to New York; she felt it only right to start at the beginning. She sped through the pages until she came to the obituaries. And stopped in shock.

It was there. She hadn't wanted it to be, but it was. It couldn't be, it just couldn't be. She'd never expected to find it on the obit pages, but she always had to look—she had to know. Now she did know, but she didn't believe it—she couldn't believe it. She just couldn't.

She read it quickly until she saw the name of the cemetery. Her heart pounding frantically, she ran from the library. She had to see it to believe it, to really believe it. Her lungs were burning and gasping furiously for air when she finally stopped at the rusted old gate. She pushed it open and walked between the rows of tombstones; suddenly, her feet stopped of their own volition in front of one—the one.

Caroline sank to her knees in front of it, screaming with the worst pain she'd ever felt. Her fingers slowly traced the letters of the name—his name—as tears streamed down her face. Joseph Lee Heywood. Joseph. Her dear, sweet Joseph. The only man she'd ever loved. The man she'd spent the past fifteen years searching for. And he'd been here the whole time.

He'd been killed—run down by a car—the morning she'd left. While she'd been on the plane to New York, he'd been lying in the street dying. The street in front of her apartment. Witnesses said he'd run from the apartment building crying, never seeing the car coming toward him. If she'd stayed in Charleston he'd be alive. They'd have made up, she'd have apologized to him, and they'd have been at the diner eating breakfast together as they had every morning. Instead, she'd left; she'd killed him by not being here. He'd come back to her and she hadn't been here. She'd never known.

That afternoon her manager arranged a frantic search party to find her. When they finally asked the librarian if Caroline had been there, she showed them the newspapers still where Caroline had left them. Confused, puzzled and worried, the policeman led them to the cemetery listed in the obituary.

There they found her, lying across the grave of Joseph Heywood. She was dead. The coroner ruled the death was by natural causes. Broken hearts never show up in autopsies.

## *All of My Life*

All of my life, I have written half a song. I wrote the music and the first verse when I was a boy (not a man) of 21, after my first heartbreak. Oh, how wretchedly my soul ached then. I prayed—begged—for death. Life was not worth living in that miserable condition. I lost all hope, faith, and joy. I did not want to endure. I did not want to feel.

Then I literally ran into you, and I felt more than I had ever imagined any human could ever feel. I didn't just suddenly believe in love at first sight. I knew it intimately. In one millisecond, my soul sang God's praise for the unexpected answer to my prayer. Instead of ending my desolate existence, he made it exultant. He sent me you. You filled my being with love, with peace, with purpose.

You trusted me, believed in me, loved me. Through all of my wild ideas and various jobs, you stuck by me. When money was in short supply, you never became frustrated or angry. When I dreamed of making something of my music, you urged us to move to New York City, where I struggled as a pianist. No matter how little I could give you, you never complained. You kept encouraging me, even when I felt like giving up. You wouldn't let me.

You often came to the club to cheer me. You were my biggest fan—my only fan. You took care of me so that I could go to my job at the bank every day and still have the stamina to go to the club every evening. You told me at least once a day that someday my name would be in lights. Every time I thought of giving up, you told me that. I couldn't give up when I looked into your eyes that shone with your love for and belief in me.

I kept my gig at the club through the 1980s, during all of the changing styles and tastes, playing the classic songs that patrons wanted to hear. I was their piano man, the one who provided the soundtrack to their lives.

They put dollars in the jar on the piano. They danced to the songs. They enjoyed their evenings at the club. They—and you—allowed me to have my music.

Oh, my darling Evelina, we were so indescribably happy for so long. When we waltzed to our wedding song at our diamond anniversary party in the spring, I felt the same overwhelming happiness I felt when I was 22 and we waltzed to that song on our wedding day. You were as beautiful to me as you were that long-ago day. You have always been beautiful to me. Oh, how much love we shared for sixty years.

You lived your wedding vows every moment of those sixty years. You never gave up on me. I could never give up on you. You were the beauty and the love in my life. My first love had become disillusioned with me, by my dreams of a music career. That wasn't practical and realistic, she said, and when I refused to abandon my music, she abandoned me. The only music I ever wrote was in the wake of that pain. I began a song of lost love and longing that I never finished. I had no need to for sixty years, because you brought me such joy.

I remember our trip to the beach the spring of our thirtieth anniversary. We strolled through the sand, laughing as the water lapped over our feet and legs. That night, I built a small fire on the beach, and we danced to nature's music as the stars twinkled. "They are smiling, Bobby. They are happy for us," you said. I will never forget your girlish giggle as I spun you into a dip and kissed you. We sat on that beach, warmed by the fire, until sunrise the next morning. We shook the sand from our shoes and walked to a diner for breakfast. What a romantic anniversary that was.

You startled me with a surprise party on my 75th birthday. I had not had a surprise party since I was five years old. You invited all our friends, and then you all came to the club that night, where the party continued. You even arranged for us to have the dance floor to ourselves for one song. The regulars got a real kick out of that. Margie Brennar told me later that she understood why I played love songs so passionately. Seeing us so in love after 53 years was all the proof she needed.

What an amazing wife you are, Evelina. Your love made me feel like a king. Your love gave me hope, peace, confidence, security, consolation, and faith. With you, everything was possible and as perfect as it could be. You didn't tolerate my dreams. You nurtured them.

I told you before our wedding about that half-written song, and you replied, "Maybe you won't ever need to finish that one. I hope you never feel such pain again." With you I never did. Pain became a distant memory.

I thought I knew heartbreak at 21. How foolish I was then. I had no idea what heartbreak feels like. I do now, Evelina. I finished that song. I had to know heartbreak as intimately as I had known love. That song could never be finished as long as we lived happily. Happiness does not inspire despair. Only one thing could. I had to lose you, my darling, in order to write that song. I knew the truest happiness with you. Now I know the rawest pain without you.

Today is your 80th birthday. I have brought you a bouquet of your favorite yellow roses, as I have done on every birthday since your 20th. I will leave them here at your grave for you to enjoy, darling. I love you.

## *Tommy*

Tommy sat alone at a corner table, his hand curled around a now-cold cup of coffee. He stared at his left hand, at his wedding band. Jenny had placed the ring on his finger exactly six months earlier. He smiled as he saw her walk toward him, her white lace train floating behind her. He had never seen a more beautiful sight anywhere, not even in the sappiest movies. Their wedding was the culmination of his dreams, of his happiness. He knew that now. He would never feel as happy again.

They had flown to Jenny's ancestral Scotland for their

honeymoon. Neither of them had ever loved another. They had waited for one another, and they loved completely—heart, soul, mind, and body. They were best friends. They shared everything—their hopes, dreams, and fears. As they sat amongst a castle ruin, three days after their wedding, Jenny had stared at the sea and said, "Our love is a real love, an eternal love, a strong love. It can survive anything." She turned and stared at him. "Can't it?"

"Of course it can, Jenny. That's not a question a man expects from his new bride on their honeymoon," Tommy smiled, trying to ignore his uneasiness.

"I know. I'm sorry. It must be the ancient history of this place, and the ghosts who live here, that are getting to me," Jenny nervously giggled.

"Let's go, then. A nice walk back to the inn will clear our minds. Come on." Tommy put his arm around Jenny and held her near as they slowly walked along the narrow dirt road.

Moments later, Jenny leaned up, kissed his cheek, and said, "I love you, Tommy. I love you. You will write that bestseller, and you will become one of the great writers of our time."

"I love you, Jenny. Your faith in me is all I need," Tommy said. He stopped walking, and shared a passionate kiss with her. Suddenly, Tommy felt her push him, and as he fell backwards, he heard the grinding sound of tires and brakes. Through the dust, Tommy saw Jenny crumpled, unmoving.

"Jenny!" he heard himself scream as he hastily crawled to her side. The driver of the car stared at Tommy in horror. He knew. He knew before he felt for her pulse that Jenny was dead.

"Get away from her! Don't touch her!" Tommy yelled, and pushed the man away from her.

Jenny had died instantly, the coroner told Tommy, and said she didn't feel anything. Tommy never believed that. Of course she had. In the moment of impact, she had felt the most excruciating pain. Jenny had known what would happen before it happened.

Tommy stared at his wedding band as his brain relived that moment. Jenny said their love was real and strong. Her last act proved that. Jenny had saved Tommy. She saved him, and sacrificed herself. Her love saved him.

She had believed in him. His first book was dedicated to Jenny.

# *Progeny of Heaven*

Emily went where she had gone every day for the past six months—to Timothy's grave. She could not stay away. If she did, it would mean that she had forsaken their eternal bond of love. Her friends had long ago given up trying to make her realize that going forward and living her own life did not mean that she had to forget Timothy. They knew she could and would never do that, just as they would not forget their friend. But she would not listen to reason, and seemed to mutate into a veritable zombie. She no longer did anything except go to the cemetery.

She sat there for hours each day, talking to Timothy, reading to him, writing in her journal—writing to and about him—and praying that God would grant her one desire: to be with Timothy again. It wasn't enough, she cried, to know that his spirit would remain with her. It wasn't enough to know that when she died, they would be reunited in Heaven. She missed his voice, his eyes, his humor, his love, his compassion. She missed *him*. Why couldn't she have him back? Why?

Timothy was her soul mate, her life force, her reason for being. Without him, she had nothing—no energy, no passion, no purpose. Without him, she didn't want to live.

She didn't want anything except Timothy. She had never known that the human heart could break so utterly, could hurt so intensely, until doctors told her that Timothy was. . . . . She couldn't even think the word, it was so abhorrent to her. How could she go on like this for—however her miserable life continued?

As if sharing her pain, the clouds opened up and shed their tears. Emily remained beside Timothy for hours, refusing to leave him alone in the cold rain. Her tears mingled with the rain as she allowed herself to touch the pain she had kept at a distance for so long. She cried until she could cry no more, until there were no more tears left. As lightening illuminated the sky and thunder roared, Emily sank to the damp, muddy ground and reached for the tombstone. Her voice hoarse, she murmured, "Please bring Timothy back," as strong arms lifted her and the world went black.

She opened her eyes, squinting at the bright sunlight that filled the room. Emily looked around at the unfamiliar furniture and walls. Where was she? Heaven? Hell? Why was she alone? She noticed her jeans and t-shirt draped across a chair, and was puzzled to find herself wearing a yellowed ruffled nightgown. Her mind screamed for answers: How had she gotten there? Would she ever see Timothy again? She had to know. She flung her legs over the side of the bed and her feet onto the floor. Her legs were weak, and she collapsed to the wooden floor.

Suddenly, the door opened, and a tall, sweat-soaked man appeared. "What are you doing?" he inquired in a Swiss French accent. "You should not be out of bed yet. You need your rest."

He picked her up and placed her on the bed as he spoke and as questions crowded her befuddled mind: "Who are you? Where am I?"

"I am a doctor, and we are in my home." He held a glass to her mouth and helped her drink the amber liquid he offered. “Drink this; it will help you to sleep. You have a fever, and you need to rest.”

“But. . . .”

“Not now. Everything will be perfect when you awaken,” he said as he pulled the covers over her.

Her eyelids felt so heavy, and she couldn’t fight the sleep that quickly dominated her. “Nothing will ever be perfect again,” she muttered.

The doctor closed the drapes, then smiled at her as he left the room. “Yes, it will, Emily. Your prayers will be answered.”

“Good morning, Emily. How do you feel?”

It was the doctor. He was sitting in a chair across the room, smiling at her. “Confused. Everything. . . .”

“Everything is just as it should be,” he interrupted. He handed her a glass of orange juice, her favorite, and told her to drink it. “Your clothes are there,” he pointed to the chair where she had seen her clothes two days earlier. “I think it is time you get dressed and join me in the parlor next door.”

He left her wondering just who he was. Why was he always so optimistic? And formal? And since when did men dress as he did, in ruffled shirts and tall boots? She quickly changed into her jeans and t-shirt, wanting to know more about this mysterious doctor.

She ran into the next room, only to stop frozen in place by the sight before her. Her heart screamed with joy, yet no sound came from her mouth; she was muted by her intense emotions. "Emily. My darling Emily."

She never felt her legs move, but she was promptly in his arms, her own holding him with all of the love and desperation she felt. "Timothy."

"I'm here, and I will always be here," he whispered as their bodies seemed to melt together.

Emily never questioned how Timothy had returned after several months; she knew that miracles defied human explanation and comprehension. All that mattered was that Timothy was with her. She had felt the worst pain conceivable without him, and now she felt the greatest happiness imaginable with him. She and Timothy were never apart, and they never took one second of time together for granted.

Emily and Timothy were completely recovered from their

ordeals, and the doctor had pronounced them both quite healthy. The wedding they had been planning when Timothy had. . .left would take place in a short while. No one would attend except their new friend, Victor, and the local priest.

Victor wanted them to be married in his garden, where he had once married the love of his life. He wanted beauty and love to result from his work, not ugliness and pain as before. When he had found Emily at the grave, pleading for Timothy to return, he knew he could help her find happiness again.

Victor had tried to talk himself out of doing it, until he read her agonized journal as she lay unconscious in the bedchamber that had gone unused for too long. He realized then that he had come back so he could help Emily find peace and hope once more. So he had carried Timothy to his home, too, where he could work in private. It was the least he could do to make up for. . . . .

His mind was forced back to the present by Emily's soft voice at his bedchamber door. She was absolutely dazzling, her long hair piled in loose ringlets, wild flowers in her hair and in her hand. The yellowed lace gown she wore, with its empire waistline, was his wedding gift to Emily, one once given to his bride. Emily pirouetted before him, just as Elizabeth had done so very many years before on their wedding day. Victor had betrayed Elizabeth by his misdeeds, but he knew that she would be pleased with the turn of events. He would pay his restitution to the world by giving Emily and Timothy the chance for a lifetime of contentment and joy.

That evening, Mr. and Mrs. Timothy Edwards were surprised when Victor announced that he was leaving, and that he wanted them to have the estate as a wedding gift. Not accepting their refusal, he handed Timothy the deed and kissed Emily's cheek before he thanked them for helping him. They were stunned. How had they helped him? He had nursed Emily and brought Timothy to her. He had done more for them than they could ever repay. "On the contrary, my friends, it is you who have given me the greatest of gifts—the chance to right an egregious wrong. I know you will remain eternally happy here."

Before they could say or do anything, he was gone, leaving them to start their new life as husband and wife. Emily waved as Victor's horse sped into the horizon and took him from view. She would never forget him and his invaluable kindness. Neither would Timothy.

Victor settled in his cabin aboard a ship nearing the arctic. He was returning to the place where he had spent more than two agonized centuries. The difference was that now he would no longer hunt ghosts from the past; he could bury them all, beginning with his own.

He sat at the small desk and opened his journal, writing what he knew would be the final entry:

*Timothy was examined this morning and is in perfect health. There are no defects in body or mind, a fact verified by the woman who became his bride today. She has remained loyal and true to him, and has welcomed him back into her life and her arms with all the passion of true love. He is the same man whom she loved and mourned—the man she calls kind, compassionate, and beautiful in body, mind, and spirit. He is concerned of nothing but her well-being and happiness, and attends to her every need. Nothing about him has changed, despite the procedure performed four months previously. Naught was different between Timothy's procedure and the one done more than 200 years prior, except one—the person resurrected was virtuous and rational prior to death, and returned to life the same. The vile creature that once terrified the world is no more; in his place is a righteous man.*

*I shall retire from the world with the peace of knowing that the horrifying, ungodly wrong done so long ago has been rectified. No one need know of my deed; it is enough that I and God know, and that Emily and Timothy will live together in the happiness which they deserve. May God grant them many years together. And may God forgive me for my former pride and wickedness, and have mercy on one who seeks clemency, though undeserved. I am evermore grateful for the brief return that has enabled me to offer this restitution.*

*Your Humble Servant,*

*Victor Frankenstein*

***Sheilah R. Craft*** is an English professor, writer, blogger, poet, artist, ardent genealogist, and book lover. Born and raised in the Midwestern United States, Sheilah was born surrounded by a close family—including several educators—books, and animals. She began reading and writing very early, and has published short stories, articles, and poems. She was literally born a writer. Her series of novels centered on the lives of one family dynasty and spanning more than two centuries began in the fall of 2012 with the first volume, Heart-Glow. The second volume, First Love Never Dies, was published in the spring of 2013. Heart Eternal is the third volume in the series. Three more volumes are planned. Soulscapes is a collection of half a dozen short stories.